ALONG THE ROADSIDE

ALONG THE ROADSIDE

LAURENCE DAVID

Photographs by Cathy David

RESOURCE *Publications* · Eugene, Oregon

ALONG THE ROADSIDE

Resource Publications
An Imprint of Wipf and Stock Publishers
199 W. 8th Ave., Suite 3
Eugene, OR 97401

www.wipfandstock.com

PAPERBACK ISBN: 979-8-3852-4323-5
HARDCOVER ISBN: 979-8-3852-4324-2
EBOOK ISBN: 979-8-3852-4325-9

1

The cycle that never ends
is a circle that always begins.

In a complete collection
every element is interconnected.

If it's in God's plan
every thread is interwoven.

He's the master of his art
whose hand does not extend too far.

To achieve the proper balance
you need to keep your distance.

A flame that's out of reach
cannot be extinguished.

You cannot close the gap
till you tie the knot.

Because our hands are tied
we let it slip away.

Working for no apparent reason
can mean it's all for nothing.

There's no shame in failing
at anything that's not true.

To what degree you're a failure
depends on how it's measured.

For failure to bring out your best
requires some measure of success.

Desperation makes a fool
of any man.

A man in desperation
is begging for something.

The head hangs low
when the shoulders bear the load.

For humiliation the final reward
is a seat of honor.

When heaven measures fame and fortune
together they add up to nothing.

What to some is bottled up
to others is an empty cup.

That cup is not full
that falls one drop short.

Though more is often better
less is sometimes best.

With simplicity we add strength
by subtracting content.

More often than not
simplicity leads to purity.

His conscience is clear
whose words are pure.

To show the way
to dignity is integrity.

By keeping your true self hidden
it's a lie you're living.

Keeping your true self hidden
can be the only safe haven.

That voice crying out of the wilderness
is from a position of peace.

Silence is without voice,
but has the face of peace.

Beyond the stillness
is absolute silence.

2

Nothing rings true
if it doesn't bear fruit.

All the seeds that fall from heaven
on earth must come to fruition.

It's only a small leap
from seed to falling leaf.

After harvest comes winter
to enjoy the fruits of your labor.

If not for the Sun,
the Seed of life would not be sown.

A life without the sun
is like a dry desert bone.

The sun comes up
with a ray of hope.

The sun going down can sometimes
open up a man's eyes.

Remember the morning sun
when the evening rain comes.

When day and night pass each other by
the sun and moon see eye to eye.

At dusk and at dawn
the sun and moon face off.

What shines like the Sun
lights up the dawn.

Through the eye of the storm
we see the face of dawn.

With the laws of nature
what was lost is recaptured.

Spring hopes to restore peace
to the summer breeze.

That there is no perfection
lies at the heart of creation.

The laws of nature were put in place
to catch the souls that fall from grace.

Not only in nature
does beauty hide its cruelty.

Not only in nature
is beauty masked by cruelty.

Beneath a spiritual overflow
is a strong undertow.

That the spiritual can transform the physical
is what we call a miracle.

The Spirit that returns to the Creator
can reverse the laws of nature.

3

Starting from nothing we go
full circle back to zero.

Your journey sets you on another course,
while the Circle brings you back to the source.

What sets the wheels in motion
is an active imagination.

The four steps of a journey are the spring,
the stream, the river and the sea.

A journey is never ending,
or a dead end.

If it's a true beginning,
there can be no ending.

To find the beginning and end
look behind and beyond.

Returning to the source
leads to a higher innocence.

The way to a better place
is by way of peace.

His way is clear
whose path is pure.

True peace is knowing what you do
leads you to the truth.

Struggling towards the truth
is enough to pull you through.

It takes many trips to the ledge
for the journey to move ahead.

To escape this endless maze
turn back the other way.

To find a way around the sun
keep rotating your position.

A doorway that's blocked
gives the illusion of being locked.

The road that's closed
drove you back home.

What a new direction may hold
is an old familiar road.

Wherever you are the Spirit
leaves the door ajar.

All but one path reaches the door,
falling one step short.

It's easy to fall short
when desire is not of the heart.

There's much to look back on
to see how far you've come.

Not knowing the beginning
you can only imagine the end.

The road approaches completion
before the journey reaches the end.

Everyone is protected from the storm
that arrives safely home.

4

The first and the last
has neither future nor past.

The Spirit brings future, past and present
together in one moment.

Seize the divine moment
that goes beyond time and space.

The time of divine inspiration
is the moment the door opens.

Time is well spent
when you seize your moment.

Time is spent in the past
when your moment has been missed.

Before a moment has passed
the time is lost.

In its haste the promise of youth
is spent before payment is due.

Make sure the days of innocence
is not a time of ignorance.

Rising above the past
means looking back from a distance.

You learn what you had
by rediscovering the past.

To recapture a moment
reach beyond the present.

Memory searches the past
for a place to rest.

Time says all that was
is what will be.

5

Only by surrendering
can anything truly begin.

Surrender is at the heart
of life in the Spirit.

Your spirit begins to live
when the soul gives in.

By surrendering to the Spirit
the soul draws near it.

The Spirit is unfolding
when the heart is surrendering.

To surrender it all
means mind, body and soul.

Surrendering body and soul
requires more than self-control.

Heart and soul are not truly free
till you surrender the mind and the body.

To win the war when you lost the battle
surrender mind and body to the soul.

In order to triumph over
pride must surrender under.

Surrender takes the position
of least resistance.

You can't pry open
a window of opportunity.

Be sure to surrender
before the open door.

Doing nothing doesn't always mean
nothing will ever happen.

To capture the Spirit in your hands
takes all the strength restraint demands.

Holding freedom in your hand
is like trying to trap the wind.

To let go of your boat
only cease to row.

The secret to wisdom
and understanding is surrendering.

The truth behind believing
lies in surrendering.

6

What is born of belief
reason can't conceive.

At the heart of true faith
is a burning desire to believe.

Innocence gives birth
to endless hope.

A Child's faith is strong
whether it's proven right or wrong.

The soul needs no proof
of what it knows to be true.

The deepest truth
needs no proof.

Faith is the only proof
when you're a world removed.

By believing you prove
that the Word is true.

Between the lines we edit out
words to erase any doubt.

The strongest faith will kill
any reason to doubt.

Faith encountered little resistance
until reason entered in.

Once the lines of faith are crossed
all hope is lost.

A house built on reason and law
cannot stand on faith.

No faith is pure
with the fear of failure.

A lack of strength
requires a leap of faith.

That man fell from grace
demands a leap of faith.

After the fall from grace
comes a leap of faith.

A true leap of faith
jumps in without thinking.

Though the mind's eye has seen it
it can't quite believe it.

What means more is when what's not seen
is still believed in.

You're lost with no hope and
then a door swings open.

Love leads the way
by the hand of faith.

Faith is the final link
in the chain of command.

7

Grace is the missing link
in the chain of command.

With the loss of innocence
came the birth of grace.

What came through grace
is sustained through praise.

Believing Christ is the source
you see no end to His grace.

Grace extends to every hand
to reach beyond body and mind.

If not for grace
death would not end in peace.

A soul is at peace
in a state of grace.

Not by withholding grace
is the soul restored to peace.

Grace gives freely
asking only to be received.

8

Love can't help but give
to a heart that would receive.

The spirit of love unfolds
before its seeds will blossom.

A love that shines clear and bright
is touched by pure Sunlight.

With nothing to replenish the soil
love bears little fruit at all.

A love that's grounded
leaves the heart confounded.

A broken heart feels love
only in part.

Ignore a love and risk
that it cease to exist.

Before love reaches the end
the spirit has already fled.

A love that walks the ledge
has reached the wall of death.

When love fell from grace
a light left the world in disgrace.

A love that died in vain
lives on in infamy.

A love that's been defeated
can still be completed.

A love is not yet complete
that doesn't chance to risk defeat.

That two come from one is the law of separation:
that two become one is the law of restoration.

What if you already have
what you've always loved?

Like the Father and Son in the Spirit are One,
the wife and husband in the flesh are one.

From the Father above
comes true Mother Love.

Pure energy and love
is the spiritual life's blood.

Love is a true blessing
whatever lie you're living.

That love is full
which embraces both body and soul.

A love that cuts deep
goes beyond the body.

Love that goes beyond the mind
has no reason or rhyme.

A love that reaches beyond death
continues to draw breath.

9

Love cannot travel far
until you take it to heart.

A heart that's true must rise above
the world it was born into.

Discover where the heart is
to find out where you started.

The struggle to escape
is one the heart can embrace.

A heart that has courage
will embrace any challenge.

At the heart of redemption
is the desire for perfection.

A heart must surrender
for the Spirit to deliver.

Encouragement strengthens the heart,
but criticism can kill the spirit.

A true gift of the heart
is when two exist as one.

A heart that remains true
can never learn not to love you.

A heart that's pure can preserve
its own true nature.

A heart that is full
is of body and soul.

To satisfy the soul
the heart must be full.

10

Where heart and soul meet
is where a seed takes root.

Restoring the soul to its place
is a return to peace.

Everything is in its place
when the soul is restored to peace.

The body must be broken
before the soul is restored.

There's only one escape from the body
for the soul to be free.

Between the body and soul
is a self-imposed exile.

From the body the soul is removed
like a hand from a glove.

What can freeze you to the bone
can also burn through to your soul.

A soul cannot be slave to anything
that's of body and mind.

A soul is lost from within
when no direction is given.

Whatever is not spiritual
weighs heavy on the soul.

The creation of hell
is for the destruction of the soul.

Satan's one obsession
is the soul's destruction.

The powers of heaven and hell
are sworn enemies for the soul.

Heaven descended into hell
to resurrect the soul.

A soul that is reborn
continues to grow and be transformed.

The soul comes of age
from its own hermitage.

The depth of the soul
reaches beyond the deepest well.

Providing for the soul
is being paid in full.

What can you satisfy the soul with,
if not the Spirit?

For the soul to cry out to the Spirit
requires the utmost in quiet.

11

Only the Spirit can restore peace
to its rightful place.

Only the soul can surrender to the Spirit, and not fear it;
only the heart can embrace the Spirit, and not fear it.

The Spirit must fight through the body
to save the soul.

The Spirit returns to the well
to replenish the soul.

Every life must return
to where its spirit was born.

The Love the Spirit began
is driven to completion.

A discerning spirit can discriminate
between love and hate.

A true spirit can discriminate
between lies and fact.

The Spirit of man is made whole
by separating body and soul.

Passion can rule the heart and mind,
but not the Spirit of man.

The Spirit dreams of peace
when the mind is fast asleep.

The Spirit flows from the source
of the unconscious.

The Spirit leaves behind no bridges burned,
and no stone unturned.

The Spirit was silent
before the Word was sent.

Though the body is just a shell,
the Spirit will live to tell.

The Spirit rises above death
and frees the body from earth.

12

It's the Spirit in prayer
that keeps the heart pure.

By purifying your prayer
you keep your heart pure.

Pure is the flower
that stems from prayer.

Pure is the shower
that springs from prayer.

A prayer was on our tongue
before the Word would come.

Prayer is the only answer
to the call to arms.

For the spiritual struggle inside
every prayer is a battle cry.

Prayer waits for the moment
when a door opens.

For a soul that waits-
a prayer of patience.

13

The dream of completion
in this life is an illusion.

By following your true calling
you avoid chasing a false dream.

The dreams that have died
lie side by side along the roadside.

What if it's all true;
the dream meant only for a fool?

One day we wake up to the fact
that the Dream was real.

Your dream and nightmare
is a glimpse of heaven or hell.

A dream is a vision
with no clear meaning.

A vision is a dream
with a clear meaning.

14

Behind the doors of perception
is an opening into vision.

By looking within
you find the door that's open.

Vision looks within
to see what lies ahead.

Vision chooses to reach out
by looking within.

Vision sees far off in the distance
by looking back at a glance.

To see a new direction
look back in reflection.

To see beyond the mind's eye
look behind the light inside.

Look beyond imagination
where the conscious mind cannot be seen.

Vision opens the mind
to see beyond reason.

A man with pure vision
can see more than the light of reason.

Vision sees a pattern
where reason says there is none.

With vision you may see a pattern
when there's no rhyme or reason.

True vision sees everything
from any position.

A gift as small as a seed
with vision can still be seen.

Illusion is what you saw
before you looked for more.

For vision to unfold
it must look past the world.

Looking out from the inside
you see a world gone mad.

To see through any lie
find the truth it hides behind.

Captured for all to see into
is the hidden nature of truth.

For those who see with their true eye,
how can a vision be a lie?

Vision that truly sees
reflects an image of peace.

Vision is best seen
as a reflection of the soul.

Vision sees the Trinity
as the heart, mind and body of the Mystery.

Vision is heaven sent
that can see beyond death.

When all the embers have died
vision can still see the light.

Behind the darkest night
there are still signs of light.

Even in the darkest night,
a glimpse of vision is brought to light.

Vision is the source of light
to a man who was blind.

A light that is truly visionary
can see its way out of obscurity.

A light that shines through
reaches the eye of the storm.

A spark of light is another star
to those who can see that far.

A light that has lost its luster
can in time regain its shine.

The hope of another light
is the next morning to the night.

Vision from an inner life
reveals a much brighter light.

By looking inside
vision reveals an inner light.

The light of illusion
has no vision.

Lost in a world of illusion
is any sense of vision.

Vision has shown time and again
why the world is an illusion.

You blindly cross over
when the lines are blurred.

What vision is clear
when the lines are blurred?

Fear is a dark vision
hiding from the sun.

Vision has little chance
in the face of blind ignorance.

Worse than wisdom crying in the streets,
is vision fast asleep.

To the eye without vision
a sign is without meaning.

To keep an open mind
don't close your eyes to the signs.

So often the eyes remain shut
until the heart is touched.

Vision that is clear and sharp
cuts to the heart.

A man with vision
can block out the night.

Once you step outside the world
the lines are no longer blurred.

A vision of the Spirit
remains true to the Image.

Vision is completed
when the veil is lifted.

15

Wisdom is a reflection
of true vision.

A man of pure vision
has an eye for wisdom.

While vision sees the Light without blinking,
wisdom knows the Truth without thinking.

True wisdom is always sound
and true vision in never blind.

A lack of vision
is the absence of wisdom.

To the mind without understanding
wisdom is without meaning.

The wisdom you can't understand
is the one that has no end.

You may discover the age old wisdom,
but long after you've grown.

The depth of wisdom
when searched is never ending.

The deepest wisdom knows
the truth is hidden.

Wisdom knows the Mystery
cannot be heard or seen.

The gift of wisdom
is a glimpse of heaven.

Silence bears a true witness
to the power of wisdom.

Wisdom cries out for justice
that results in peace.

Wisdom accepts a season of peace,
knowing its time will cease.

Wisdom that ends with reason
will always draw the wrong conclusion.

Discover true wisdom
before reason enters in.

The truth behind wisdom
lies not with reason.

You need the deepest wisdom
to reach beyond reason.

The way to the deepest wisdom
won't be found within reason.

By not seeing beyond reason
you won't know the source of wisdom.

The search for true wisdom
begins and ends far beyond reason.

16

Be sure to rise above reason
before you fall into confusion.

To rise above reason
goes beyond any question.

To rise above reason
is to reach beyond the system.

To reach beyond the mind
break free from the constraints of reason.

Though he's free a man's mind
keeps him imprisoned in space and time.

All the lies of reason
are contained in one false system.

What has no reason or rhyme
is no system of the mind.

That the truth makes no sense
confounds the laws of reason.

Anything but what the truth is
can be disputed.

Leave it to man's reason
to reach the ultimate in ignorance.

Arrogance is the highest
form of ignorance.

On the edge of darkness
reason falls into madness.

In the mind temptation
can give rise to obsession.

Fear in the hands of reason
is twisted into an angry demon.

A single thought can be the cause
when all hope is lost.

Clouds of reason continue to form
even after the storm has gone.

To the Spirit reason represents
the wind of resistance.

It's a spiritual wind
that flies in the face of reason.

A quiet voice inside
can silence the mind.

It may be a blessing-
the inability to reason.

Inspiration touches the heart
before reason makes a conscious effort.

To ponder is to reason,
but to wonder is to imagine.

Above reason and religion
is the divine imagination.

Imagination is paralyzed
when inspiration runs dry.

The worst combination of reason
is religion and no imagination.

17

The truth in the hands of reason
is twisted into false religion.

To rise above religion
break free from the confines of reason.

It's easy to twist religion
into an excuse for sin.

Any sin in the name of religion
can be justified in the end.

Anything that brings a man to ruin
in the name of God is religion.

Religion fails to illuminate
the light of the Spirit.

The one true Church of the Holy City
celebrates the visionary trinity.

Worse than the marriage of business and art
is the union between church and state.

Religion and government has proven
to be a lethal combination.

18

To conquer the world
is to capture its spirit.

What inspires war between nations
is the art of retaliation.

Pride will topple every
earthly kingdom and throne.

Anger has power
but only for destruction.

Evil has direction
but only towards destruction.

Hatred is a product
of anger and fear.

Despair is a product
of fear and doubt.

Hate that makes a fist
holds you in its grip.

Revenge is a song
better left unsung.

Love reacts to hate
not by turning away.

Peace is to be had
in the aftermath.

Peace in the eyes of man
is nothing but an illusion.

In a time of war
peace requires more prayer.

Behind a prayer for peace
is a wall of silence.

Behind the face of war
is a vacant stare.

Against the call to arms
is no resistance to peace.

A friend to war and chaos
is the sworn enemy of peace.

In the face of destruction
killing is not an option.

For the true Christian violence
is not an option in self-defense.

Only with passive resistance
can you defuse the violence.

The last line of defense
is a wall of silence.

To the soul there's no earthly war
worth killing and dying for.

With the curse of rage
the soul is ravaged.

Regardless of the world's struggle,
the soul is embroiled in its own battle.

The wounds of a spiritual battle
are felt in body and soul.

Pray that the battle in the soul
doesn't cause the body to fall.

For some the spiritual struggle
is body against soul.

Satan takes the stance
of greatest resistance.

Not every spiritual battle
is between good and evil.

In any kind of war
the lines become blurred.

By giving up the fight
you surrender to defeat.

To restore the soul
is worth any battle.

Though it's a continual struggle
the soul accepts the battle.

Only heart and soul
will embrace the hidden struggle.

19

Only through humility
can humanity approach divinity.

Only through humility
could divinity embrace humanity.

The ultimate sacrifice
chose death to give life.

The deepest sacrifice
lies beneath the surface.

A gift from heaven on earth
appears to have little worth.

What was easily dismissed
could be sorely missed.

What in the world seems necessary
to God may be contrary.

Whatever God asks
has been blessed.

Heaven showers a man with gifts
to be given back up to Him.

For the sake of Jerusalem,
God forgave them before they would forsake Him.

God rewrote His Law in sand
with His own right hand.

The one true promise that is given
is the kingdom of heaven.

Only One remains true
to the promise of truth.

There's only One whose every promise
will come to pass.

There's only One that can make
something happen from nothing.

With everything but One
there's an imperfection.

All but One will reach the door,
and still fall short.

20

Rushing headlong towards death
we hope to catch our breath.

A moonlit path
lights the way to death.

Before the fire of hell
is the chill of death.

Death is one truth
that cannot be refuted.

The whole story is never told
until after the epilogue.

It all ends in defeat
but the final victory.

Thanks to death
there's life to resurrect.

To venerate life
is to vilify death.

That death ends in peace
is as certain as the course of any disease.

What doesn't end in peace
is not yet complete.

That death returns to life means
the circle is complete.